A Young Man's Wisdom

Rueben Nathaniel Brock

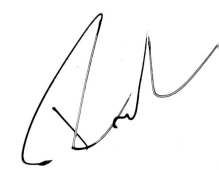

A Young Man's Wisdom

Copyright © 2010 by Rueben Brock

ISBN 9780615428420

Printed in USA by 48HrBooks

This book is dedicated to the memory of my father, the late William B. Brock.

A Young Man's Wisdom

Part One

Introduction

I've always known that growing up without a father had an impact on my life. It wasn't until my son was born that I really began to understand the impact that a father has on a young boy. Every aspect of my son's experience is shaped by the way I talk and act. When I realized how important the messages I send are to his development, it made me realize that the messages I was sent as a child had a profound impact on me.

Much of what I am writing is about my own story. In that sense, I suppose this book is my exploration of the messages I was sent by my father before he passed away. In a more general sense, this book is about the typical messages that society sends little boys about what it means to be a man. It's about the messages I would hope that I am sending my little man-in-training. I hope that I have been sending them by living them. Just in case, I am writing them down.

I would like to thank Will, Danny, and Matt. These are the men with whom the fat was chewed that became this book. I would like to thank my daughter, Dominique. She inspired me to be the man I hope I will become one day. I thank my son for accepting the burden of being a better version of me. Being a man is no easy business. Being my son is probably just unfair. Most of all, though, I have to thank my mother. She taught me the lessons no one else was there to teach. She made me the man I am. For that, I owe her more than I can pay.

Anyone who knows me knows that I love my mother something awful. But, to be honest, she won't like that I've written this book. My mother is a very private person, and some of the stories I share in this book are her stories. But, my stories are her stories. My story of strength is also her story of pain. My story doesn't exist without hers. My hope is that in telling my story, I can give my kids a different truth. Maybe others reading this will see a different truth as well. Hopefully, my mother will believe that it's worth it.

January 7, 1983

I've always said that my life began on January 7, 1983. I was seven years old. It's the first day I can vividly remember, and I remember it like it was yesterday. My brother and sister and I were in the basement watching television. *Knight Rider*. It's strange that I can remember what television show was on, because I can't remember which shows I watched last week. Still, twenty-seven years ago I was watching *Knight Rider*. My dad came home from work late in the evening, and he and my mom were talking. I remember that the conversation seemed loud, but that wasn't anything that would cause alarm—just a normal evening at the Brock house.

Then there was the gunshot. I'd never heard a real gunshot before, but somehow, I knew what it was. It was so loud. My mom ran down the steps and yelled for us to get out of the house. As she rushed us into the car, I tried to make sense of all the confusion. Almost instantly the police and ambulance arrived at the house. In my seven-year-old mind, it seemed to me that perhaps my father must have attacked my mother and that's why she ran. As the police were walking into my house, I remember that my instinct was to go help protect my father, who I imagined was now under attack by the authorities.

I remember that as we sat in our car not attempting to go anywhere and yet not getting out of the car, our neighbors invited us into their home. That's when it dawned on me that something really bad had happened. I knew, even at my young age, that those particular neighbors didn't like my family much. It was the first time I'd been in their house, so something had to be wrong for them to invite us in. It wasn't until days later that I learned that the gunshot I heard that night was in fact from my father's gun. He had shot himself. I'm not convinced that anyone ever actually told me that. I only remember my mother explaining to us that daddy was in the hospital and that they could have saved him, but he would not have been the same. That's how I found out that my father was gone.

I always say that my life began that night. I say it because in a way, the person I became was born that night. I'm sure there are lots of people in the world who would love to be able to define the moment in their lives when everything changed. To be able to pinpoint that magical moment when the earth cracked and the stars aligned and the path of their lives changed forever. For me, it's easy. However, that defining moment, oddly enough, didn't come the night my father shot himself. Instead, it came days later. My mother, my grandmother, my sister Laila, and I were sitting at my grandmother's kitchen table. My mother was doing Laila's hair and drinking a cup of tea. I can't remember where my brother, William, was. The grown-ups were talking, as adults sometimes do, with the assumption that the kids aren't paying attention or don't understand. My grandmother and my mother were attempting to make sense of what had happened. They reasoned that William would need the most help, because he was the oldest and would understand what had happened. And, they said, Laila is the baby. Rueben will be okay.

Rueben will be okay.

It was as if they had said I was cut off from all nurturing, love, and support hence forth and forever. I can't remember, now, which one said it or the exact words used. But I know what I heard. I know what I internalized. It was that moment that defined my childhood. Not hearing a bullet go through my father's brain. Not my father's death itself. Those events weren't tangible to me. They were abstract ideas far enough removed from the core of me that they did not so much shape my view of things to come. But there at my grandmother's kitchen table, I knew my life had changed. In that moment, I felt as lonely as a seven-year-old could feel, despite being surrounded by everyone who loved me most. I was on my own. As the years went by, I would internalize that idea even more. At that moment, though, I only knew that my mother needed me to be okay. I would make that my job. Independent. Self-sufficient. Strong. It was a tall order for a seven-year-old, but it's a role I learned to accept.

The way that I internalized that role was to never appear weak. Somewhere in my young mind, I decided that it was my responsibility to never need anything from anyone. Of course at that age, my thoughts were less clear. I didn't know that I thought this. Actually understanding my thoughts came years later. Nonetheless, I learned to smile at all costs. I learned to be strong, no matter what. In short, I learned to shut down my feelings. I became cold. I remember that people used to say that I was always smiling. What they didn't know was that I had trained myself to smile. My smile was my hiding place for my sadness, my fear, and my anger. On the surface, I probably seemed to be a happy kid. I played sports. I was well liked. I had plenty of friends. Compared to my brother, who wore his emotions on his sleeves and got into every bit of trouble imaginable, I was surely a model kid. But behind my ever-present smile was a scared kid with nowhere to hide from his thoughts.

In my mind, I became a man that day at my grandmother's house. I became the man of the house. Irrational as that thought might have been, it was real to me. Every message that I had received about manhood in the first seven years of my life became a fixed part of my psyche. There was a part of me that stopped growing. My struggle to undo or revise those thoughts has been a twenty-year process, and it may very well take a few more years to get it right.

I Really Hate to Lose Something

When I think back on my childhood, it probably sounds like a country song. You know . . . the dog dies and the old man skips town. Nothing goes right. Only in my life, it wasn't a song; it was reality. From around the age of five to the age of seven, I saw more death than many people see in a lifetime. My aunt died. My grandparents died. And in classic country song fashion, my dog got hit by a bus a few days after my father shot himself. I went from being a happy-go-lucky kid in an affluent family to a lonely little fatherless child in a family desperately trying to survive.

All those deaths take a toll on a kid after awhile—they play with your mind. I imagine that anyone who has experienced a lot of death can understand the feeling I'm trying to express, but having my father leave me the way he did was probably the toughest to deal with. If your father dies of cancer, you can at least focus your anger and frustration on cancer. That's what took your father from you. If a man in the streets kills your father, you have the man in the street to blame. Your relationship with your father and the way you view him never really has to change. But my father chose to die. In a sense, he chose to leave me. The man that was supposed to love me chose to leave me when the going got tough. That reality changes things. I was both attempting to remember him with love and also attempting to wrap my mind around the idea that he didn't see fit to stick around for my family and me. When people talk about an estranged relationship with their father, I remind them that they at least have someone to be estranged from. Estranged relationships can be mended, but I don't have that opportunity.

The way that I dealt with all of that death was to learn not to attach myself to people. Caring about someone represented a potential loss. Anyone that I chose to love was yet another person who could possibly leave me. That was my fear; a fear that overwhelmed me then and sometimes overwhelms me now. Loss, for me, is painful beyond imagination, so I learned to be extremely selective about whom I gave that power to. After all, if my father could leave me, I considered it foolish to think some the girl I was dating would stick around for long.

The problem with this line of thinking is that others rarely understand how important they are to me. In those instances when I do choose to love someone, they become a fixture in my heart and mind. When someone makes it past that pretend smile, and truly sees me, it's because I have chosen to trust them and to believe that they'll stay with me. Most people don't understand that. A teenage romance is, for most, just a young romance. These things come and go; they're not intended to be permanent in most cases. Casual friendships, too, are as fragile as thin glass. However, on the occasions when I have chosen to put my heart into something or someone, it's because I want it to last. People are often confused about how and why I seem to get so attached to things that might appear to be meaningless. The answer is simple. I really hate to lose something.

Soul Shadows

If you've ever had a song stuck in your head, you know how annoying it can be. It plays over and over again, relentlessly. Most of the time you know the song or at least parts of it. You hear something catchy on the radio, and it sticks. You sing it for a while, and then it goes away. We've all been there. But when I was about fourteen years old, I had a different experience.

I was an average teenager, listening to Run DMC, New Edition, Eric B. & Rakim, and whatever else was playing on black radio at the time. But there was this song in my head that I couldn't get out. It wasn't some popular song from that time; I didn't know what it was, really. I only knew I had heard it before, and I needed to hear it again. It's like this song was calling me.

I figured out, somehow, that this song in my head had to have come from the days when my father would listen to music on Sunday mornings. My dad would play his jazz records, and we would sit around and listen. At the time, I probably felt like it was torture, just like my kids do now, when I turn up the old jazz records and turn off the television. But he would play those records loud and long, and my sister and brother and I would sit there and not pay much attention. We were babies. We were oblivious. Nonetheless, years later, I had one of those songs stuck in my head.

As my mother had long since put those records away, along with every other tangible memory of my father, I hadn't heard those songs in at least seven or eight years. But with this song stuck in my head, I figured that the only way to get it out was to hear it again. So I did the only thing I thought made sense—I pulled out all of my dad's old records. I had no idea which song, which album, or even which artist I was looking for. The song titles and artists' names on the covers meant absolutely nothing to me. So I just started at the top of the stack listened to all of them. As the music played, a floodgate opened, and years of memories started pouring back into my conscious memory. I listened to John Coltrane and Oscar Peterson, to Yusef Lateef and Joe Sample. With every song came another memory of my father. I sat there in the kitchen, reading old album covers, tears streaming down my face, finally remembering my father. I remembered things we had done and things he had said. Before that moment, I could really only remember one day, one memory.

I remembered that life-changing day like it was yesterday, but before this moment everything else had been a blur. To me, the craziest part was that there were songs I could remember, line for line, note for note. Songs that, before that day, I would have sworn I'd never heard before.

I was determined to find the song that had led me to the records in the first place. It took a while, but I finally found it: *Soul Shadows* by the Crusaders. Bill Withers sang on it. It was a song about how the old jazz greats had left the shadows of their souls behind for us. As I listened to it, I knew my father had done the same thing. He had left behind his love for music, and when I found it, I found him. In searching through that music, I had reconnected with my father.

After that, I searched my house for memories of him. I began to search for answers and understanding about his death. I was pretty much on my own to get answers because his death was not discussed in my house. And, in my own way, I did find my answers. I found the wounds that I never even knew I had, and they began to heal. I grieved my father's death for the first time. I went to his grave and said good-bye. It took some time to finally come to terms with the confusion and pain I had stirred up with those old records. But when it was all said and done, one thing was for sure—I wanted to be like my father.

The Breakdown

The newfound connection to my father wasn't all good. Accepting my connection to my father also meant accepting that I had lost a pretty important part of my life, a thought that took its toll on me. Without my realizing it, my father's choice began to shape my view of the world. More importantly, it began to shape my view of myself. I began to see every disappointment I had ever experienced as a reflection of my own faults. My father left me. In response, I rarely got close to anyone for fear they, too, would leave me. Those whom I did get close to became so important to me that they could rarely live up to the expectations I placed upon them, and when they inevitably failed me, I took it as a judgment of my own worth.

That cycle of thinking took on a life of its own at some point. If I was close to no one and could trust no one to not leave me, it must stand to reason that it was because I was not good enough to be close to anyone. I was taught to be the best, so being "not good enough" was unacceptable. If I was not able to live up to my own standards, perhaps I was not fit to live. Depression set in. It hit me hard. Many would be surprised to hear that, because I had become so good at hiding my sadness. But behind my smile was a constant question. Should I live? After all, my father had chosen not to. My life seemed to suggest a pattern, where nothing went right. By my logic, it was a strong argument for ending my life. I used to say that there was a constant battle being fought in my head: On the one side, there was a high-functioning young man, ambitious, well spoken, and educated. On the other, there was a tortured and lonely soul wanting only to stop the pain.

Realizing I needed assistance in order to sort out this battle, I began seeking help with this issue at around age 19. I went to a counselor. Because I was a clean-cut and well-spoken young man, the counselors I saw often dismissed my issues. They could scarcely understand how a kid who appeared to do so well could report feeling so bad. It didn't add up. But I kept asking for help, and occasionally, someone would listen. Still, talking to people about my feelings rarely helped me. I didn't yet understand my thoughts, so I couldn't explain them in a way that would shed light on the real problem.

It wasn't long before depression and anxiety began to win the battle. It became harder and harder to hide my symptoms. I could no longer control my thoughts. Doctors began to suggest that my mental health could only be controlled through medicine. I gave it a try—anti-depressants, anti-anxiety medications . . . the list goes on. They tried everything, but nothing seemed to work. Doctors were often baffled by my story. They could not explain how I could function so well and yet so poorly at the same time? I could articulate my symptoms perfectly, yet I appeared to be completely healthy.

The battle waged on for a number of years, and as the attempts to fix me failed, the depression and anxiety got worse. I felt control of my mind slipping away. When I was medicated enough to control my depression and anxiety, I couldn't think clearly. When the doctors reduced the medication enough to allow me to think as quickly and creatively as I usually did, my symptoms were crippling. The balance that the doctors had hoped to find seemed out of reach. The battle seemed impossible to win.

I remember my thought process. If I could not control my thoughts, I'd never live the life I wanted to live. If I couldn't live the life I wanted to live, I didn't want to live at all. And that was that. In my mind, it was a rational thought. My father had made the choice, and the family had somehow survived. It could be done. My only reservation was that it seemed to be unfair to put my mother through the pain of losing a child after already suffering the pain of losing a husband. Still, I knew she was strong. Not having to constantly help me would outweigh the loss. The decision was made: I would commit suicide.

At that point, I had been collecting all of pills from the myriad of trials of different medications that doctors had prescribed me. I had always known that suicide was a possibility, and so I kept these pills as part of a contingency plan. In my head, I planned out the act. I knew my mother's work schedule. If I took all of my pills right when she left for work, I could sit in my room and die long before she returned. I chose the day. I didn't need to say any good-byes—I assumed my passing was for the best. My only worry was that I time it so that my mother didn't have to see me die. I thought that, given our family's history, this would be too much. As long as I was long gone by the time she came home, I thought it would be okay.

When my mother left for work that day, I sat in my room with the lights out, mentally preparing to carry out my decision. I remember feeling relief. I would no longer have to battle with my thoughts and emotions. I would no longer be burdened with the feeling of disappointment that had taken over my life. *It would all end right now*. And with that thought, I began to take pills. One at a time at first, then handfuls. There were hundreds. I took all I could stomach. Then I sat on my bed and thought of what I'd say if I got to see my father.

Before I could fully process that thought, I was interrupted. There was a noise downstairs. My mother had come home. Realizing that I had miscalculated my mother's schedule for that day, I had a decision to make. I was sitting silently in my room, knowing that she would never think to look for me. There was also the chance that she would need me for something, call me for dinner, have a story about her day to tell me. She could come into my room just in time to watch me die. I couldn't do this to her. She had been there for my father's death—I couldn't make her suffer that twice. But telling her what I'd done meant inviting an intervention. I had to decide. Live or die? For my mother's sake, I chose life. I reluctantly went downstairs and told her. I did not want to live, yet I did not want to make her witness my death. She rushed me to the hospital, where they pumped my stomach. They told me that the amount of medication that was in my stomach would have killed me if she hadn't come home when she did. My mother had saved my life.

The Breakthrough

I spent a week in the psych ward after that day. As I walked around the hospital, surrounded by severely mentally ill people, I found that the doctors, once again, did not know what to do with me. I was unlike the picture of mental illness. Yet, clearly, I was not well. In that moment, my sadness was not due solely to a chronic mental illness; I had failed to accomplish my goal. I was left to continue this battle that I had hoped to end.

I returned home to my mother's house, after my stay at the hospital, determined to succeed on the second attempt. But constant supervision and a lack of motivation left me little opportunity to act. I spent most days lying on my mother's living room floor. She would go to work and return home only to find me sitting in the exact spot where she had left me in the morning. My mother, fearing that my fragile mental health could not stand any pressure, babied me for a bit, but that didn't last long.

My mother is old school. She believes in being self-sufficient. She believes in working hard. She didn't like a messy house. She didn't like my friends to be gathered at the house when she came home from a hard day's work. What she hated most of all was to go off to work, single-handedly taking care of the household expenses, while another adult sat on her floor wasting his life away. One day, after work, I could see in her eyes that her frustration had gotten the better of her, and she could no longer hold her tongue. Her angry outburst undoubtedly changed my life. Standing in the doorway, seeing me lying where I'd been lying for days on end, she gave me an ultimatum, "That's it. Get up." I assumed she only meant get up from the floor and maybe clean up a bit. She clarified. "You're not sitting on my floor anymore. If you want to waste your life away, you will have to do it somewhere else. I can't watch it anymore." She explained that she was no longer willing to support my life until I was ready to support myself. Her rules were simple: get a job; save money for a place of my own; get back into college, which I had dropped out of the year before. Otherwise, get out.

Hearing my mother, who had never before turned on me, say these things was painful. But you don't argue with my mother, so I did what she told me. I got a job at the local Wal-Mart. I applied to be readmitted to the University of Pittsburgh, where I'd been taking classes previously. Without knowing where this path would lead, I went forward. Because I had always been good at presenting myself as happy, most people I met would have had no idea I had recently experienced so much pain. I faked it. Before long, though, I realized that I actually started to feel better. I studied at-risk youth and psychology. I figured out that I was not quite as odd as I thought I was. I figured out that, in fact, I had managed to avoid many of the pitfalls that people with similar experiences fall into. I figured out that I had actually done quite well, all things considered. I found that I had the ability to relate to people who were struggling, in a way that many cannot. Before long, I began to excel. I had found my place. I had found my purpose.

I have come to believe that my struggles were preparation for the life I was meant to live. I have dedicated my life to helping other people navigate their struggles, whatever they may be. I realized, along the way, that I have an insight into people's pain that can only be gained by knowing pain on a deeply personal level. Many of my colleagues in counseling and psychology understand internal struggles from a strictly academic standpoint. I, on the other hand, know these struggles personally. It is a strange gift to have, but I wouldn't trade it for anything.

I have, over the years, pieced together the realization that traumatic stress and extreme anxiety made my problems appear. I discovered this because as I got older, I had bouts of depression far more infrequently than in my youth. Still, when things got to be hectic in my life, in moments of crisis, my depression and anxiety would resurface. Then they would go away for a time, and I would begin to believe that they had left me for good, only to be corrected by reality now and again.

Realizing the cause also helped me to control it. I figured out that the best way to make my symptoms go away was to control my stress. That's often a difficult task because I don't deal with stress well. Stress affects me physically. I become tired. I don't eat. My mind races. I get dizzy. And if it gets too bad, the real problems begin. But, I discovered if I calm myself before that point, they stay away.

Once I had learned to control my mental health to a greater and greater degree, I was able to, once again, focus on my original goal of being a good man. After all, I was, at that point, already a father. I wanted to be the best man that I could be. With no other role model, I looked to the only example I knew: my father.

Part Two

Long Shadows

Perhaps because of the way my father died, or perhaps because of how he had attempted to live, people rarely talk to me about my father. When they are brave enough to mention him at all, people generally only tell me about the fond memories they have of my father and the things he did for them. He was a community activist of sorts. He was a businessman. He was, for a time, a preacher. People tell me these stories of my father's life as if he were a saint. They speak in hushed tones. They give me looks of admiration and reverence as they tell me, "I knew your father," and "He got me a job down at the…" and "Your father was a good man." Growing up in the shadow of these stories with nothing to balance them against, led to an almost mythical place for my father inside my mind. The memories and made-up truths that I packed into my brain became my blueprint for manhood. In order to be a man, I must be like my father, I thought. The problem with this blueprint was that I didn't really know my father; I knew only the stories. I knew the praises and the admiration. To me, my father was perfect, so to be a man meant to be perfect—to be everything to everyone. The pearls of wisdom that I remember my father giving me as a child became my gospel. No one was likely to tell me that my father had owed him twenty bucks from a poker game or that he had cheated on them in high school, so I was left with the notion that he had never done any of these things. This perception, along with the fact that he was taken from me at such a young age, left me with only one single complaint: He was absent. He had not stuck around long enough to teach me how to talk to girls. He taught me how to fight, but he didn't teach me when to fight. He never got around to teaching me to toss a baseball. He wasn't there for my first trumpet recital or my college graduation. He didn't teach me to shave or why it's not okay to cuss around grown-ups. Those were lessons I'd have to learn elsewhere. As I grew up, my singular goal in life was to right that wrong. I would be the perfect father. I would be present for my children.

Superman

There's a line in *Superman* where Lois is falling from a building and Superman swoops down to catch her. He says, "Easy Miss. I've got you." Her response is logical: "You've got me? Who's got you?" It occurred to me not long ago that my teaching my son to be a man is much like Superman catching Lois. I was left here by my father, to do what good I may see fit to do. Infinite abilities with no model to observe in order to know the right paths to choose. Unlike Superman, though, I have no crystals in my bedroom that might shed light on the path that lay ahead of me. I am teaching my son to be a man, and yet, who taught me?

That is not to say that I was never taught a single thing. Quite the opposite is true. I vividly remember the little tidbits of wisdom my father attempted to impart to my brother and I. How to fight honorably (the fight isn't over until you've won); how to respect your mother (pummel anyone who speaks against her); family comes first (if you're brother's in the back alley fighting, you'd best go out and help). These are all lessons I remember my father teaching. Still, my father died when he was only 31 years old. As I reached, and then passed that age myself, a couple of profound truths hit me. First, I realized that I hadn't truly started to understand life until well into my thirties. My newfound wisdom only convinced me that I didn't know much at all. Second, I realized that if this first fact were true, then it would also stand to reason that my father, in all his infinite wisdom, didn't know all that much about manhood himself when he died. The lessons I remember him teaching me were the lessons of a man in his late twenties who had lived his youth on the mean streets of Pittsburgh. It suddenly occurred to me that I had outgrown my father's lessons; I had been living on a young man's wisdom.

This understanding didn't hit me all at once. The realization that I had surpassed my father's wisdom came slowly. After all, I had grown up with the idea that my father was perfect, and accepting that he was not was a struggle in itself. Still, I'm a relatively inquisitive and introspective person. I tend to analyze things. As I went about the walk that was my life and attempted to apply my father's lessons, I began to encounter times when my father's logic did not seem to make sense. This was especially true as I moved from young man to father, and my own fatherly intuition led me to question the instructions my father had given me in certain situations. With this realization in mind, I began to question not just one or two of the lessons, but all of them.

Lesson #1: Be the Best

There is this idea within the black community, or at least within parts of it, that in order to succeed, we must be better than our white counterparts. Being as good as them would not be sufficient to overcome the racial barriers that we inevitably face in everything we do. In my house, the lesson was no different. I remember heading out the door on the way to school as a child on my first day of kindergarten. I remember my father instructing me, no, requiring me to be three times as good as the kid next to me because twice as good was not going to be good enough. As I think back on it now, I have to wonder what exactly I was supposed to be better at. Naptime? The ABCs? Still, the message was clear. Be the best. No options. I can understand now, with an adult mind, what he was attempting to do for me. As a child, all I felt was pressure and fear. Because he was not around long enough to expound upon his original statement at a point when my mind could process it on a different level, what I ended up internalizing was the intense pressure to succeed that I felt that day. Only it went far beyond the racial context that he had originally put it in. The pressure to be the best became an overall fear of failure manifested as anxiety. I became a workaholic.

Of course, I didn't start there. I started out as a typical kid who didn't want to live up to his potential. I didn't try. I didn't care. After all, my father had created a measuring stick and failed to show it to me, so there was no way for me to know if I ever measured up. In the beginning, I chose to not make the attempt. To the frustration of most of my teachers, I did only what I needed to in order to get by. Excellence felt out of my reach. That is, until one day when a switch was flipped in my mind, and I decided to succeed at life. I imagine every boy has a moment when he decides to be a man. Little did I know then, though, that all those childhood lessons were still directing my steps. My desire for success was driven by the exact same notion that led my charge toward mediocrity. That invisible measuring stick that my father had created in me was still my goal. The only difference was that somewhere in my mind I had decided that I wouldn't sleep until I reached it.

In my professional career, I have worked with a few young women with eating disorders. What I have found about them is that, in many cases, they have this imaginary picture of a perfect woman inside their head. When they look in the mirror, it's as if they don't only see themselves. They see themselves standing naked beside this imaginary (and perfect) woman. Faced with that daily comparison, they are driven to constant anxiety. That's me. There is an imaginary man in my head that I compare myself to. I know who he is; I even know that, in reality, he wasn't perfect. In my head, though, he was a mythical and magical hero. In my mind, there is a way for me to measure up. In reality, it is impossible.

Lesson #2: We Are Our Work

When I think about the memories I have of my father, I realize that they all involve work. I can remember him coming home from his job, late at night, and saying goodnight to my brother and I who had long since gone to bed. In the mornings, we'd sometimes see him heading off to work, suit on, briefcase in hand. Most days, seeing him going to work and coming home from work was the only contact we had with him.

I'm guessing the phenomenon isn't unique. That's the stereotypical idea of a hardworking man. The images we see of what we call "good men" are usually related to work. It's as if that's all a guy has to do to be considered a good man. A good man is a man that works hard. A family man is a man that provides for his family by working. A jobless man is a no-good man. These are the ideas that popular media and society in general tell us make sense.

But, at least in the United States, it goes even further than that. Not only is work connected to a man's worth, but a man's work is his worth. In American culture, a man's work is his identity. There is something to be said for the virtue of a strong work ethic. I believe that a hardworking man is far more useful than a lazy man. The problem with connecting manhood to work so strongly is that nothing else matters. It's like a weighted exam—if one question is worth 90 percent of the test, you can essentially skip all of the rest of the questions. The same is true of the common view that a man is his work. Men grow up thinking this way and tend to forget that they are needed in other areas of life. My father undoubtedly felt that he was providing my siblings and I with exactly what we needed by working long hours and making enough money to afford us the comforts of life. But if I had to choose one more moment with him or one more dollar from his savings, my choice would be easy. That statement sounds cliché to most, but when it's your life, the cliché becomes reality.

Lesson #3: Emotion is Weakness

I have to be honest. I didn't learn this lesson from my father. He was gone much too early to have been the one to teach me this lesson in a way that I can remember. But this lesson came from everywhere. My mother. My friends. Society. Everyone seems to agree with the notion that boys aren't supposed to cry. When a little girl falls and scrapes her knee, it is expected that there will be a display of emotion. Tears will fall. Screaming will ensue. When a girl is afraid, she is permitted to show that fear. When a girl is happy, she is permitted to jump for joy, cry and shout, and show her happiness in whatever way she chooses. Boys are not given this freedom. When boys fall down, they are told, from a very young age, to get up and dust themselves off. When a boy cries, he is made fun of by his friends and scolded by his elders. Boys don't cry.

I can remember being a young boy and being disciplined by my mother. In the days before my father passed, being disciplined by my mother was a joy. My brother and I used to pretend to cry while holding back our laughter, when my mother used to whip us. On most occasions, whatever mischief we had gotten into simply required a warning that our father would be home soon. That was enough. But on the occasion that our boyish behavior merited immediate attention (i.e., my mother got so frustrated that she decided not to wait) the experience became a double joy for my brother and I. We not only got the relief of knowing that there was no longer a need for our father to intervene, thereby relieving us of the bona fide butt whipping that would result, but we also got the added fun of fooling our mother into thinking she had sufficiently punished us with her sad attempts at beating us properly. We used to practice our screams and cries, attempting to perfect our craft. But I also remember the first time she whipped us after our father died. My brother and I, fully prepared to appease her with pre-rehearsed tears and screams, were shocked. My thought in that moment was, "Wait a minute. This actually hurts!" It was as if my father's strength had been passed on to my mother with his dying breath. She had become the father.

That arm strength was not the only change. Every bit of the typical manly strength that I had seen in my father was somehow passed to my mother. She never showed fear. She never showed emotion period. Affection was an oddity. To hug was unheard of in my house. To cry was unacceptable. My sister, being the baby, was given a bit of freedom to be a typical young girl. But my expressions of fear or sadness were always met with that age-old phrase: If you want to cry, I'll give you something to cry about. The message was clear. Boys don't cry. Girls are allowed, but will be seen as weaker for it. My mother, being both the man and the woman of my house, would follow the rules of manhood.

I can remember seeing my mother cry only twice in my childhood. The first was my father's funeral. The second was in my teenage years. My mother had gone back to school, and she was studying to be a nurse. She didn't get the required grade on an important test and would therefore have to retake the course. I remember her sitting in the living room, devastated by this setback. For the first time since my father's death, my mother openly cried. I was in shock.

Emotion like that was so strange in my house that I didn't know how to handle it. I wanted so badly to help my mother. Of course, being the strong woman that she was, she would not allow me to console her, which was somewhat of a relief. I didn't have the tools to help her. A half-hearted attempt at a hug was all I could offer.

That atmosphere is probably not unique to my house. The idea of being emotional incites fear among men. Men don't hug. Men don't show sadness. Men are limited to expression of anger as the acceptable emotional outburst. In every work, academic, and social settings I have ever been in, the males have been expected to stifle all emotion or be considered feminine. As a child, I never questioned this idea. I had no reason to. As an adult, I began to wonder if it was healthy.

Lesson #4: Demand Respect

Respect is an interesting concept, especially among men. What I have learned over the years is that, among men who are used to having nothing, respect tends to become a commodity. Men with nothing else to live for will die for respect. They will fight for it, even kill for it. To many men, the idea of being disrespected boils the blood. It is instant cause to use force. It is justification for a great many foolish things. Go into any impoverished neighborhood and tell a tale of disrespect. You are not likely to find a man who will not assure you that the wrong must be righted immediately. I can remember being a very young boy and listening to my father tell me these rules. Never let a man disrespect you or your family. Defend your family at all costs. Nothing comes between a man and his family. A family stands together.

These rules all make perfect sense at face value. It is the application of these rules that becomes problematic. I imagine that these rules originated in a bygone era when the physical protection of family and home were daily necessities. For the most part, that life is not a reality anymore. Yet the ideas still prevail among men.

I remember one childhood day when, as was the case on many a day, my older brother got into a fight with one of the neighborhood boys. Being the only black family in the neighborhood, this was not an odd occurrence. On this particular day, the other boy must have gone home to his father and told him that my brother had gotten the best of him. As this was unacceptable to the boy's father, the man saw fit to walk his boy to my father's home, knock on the door, and demand that the two boys fight again. Of course, my brother, who was probably six or seven at the time, hadn't wanted to fight the first time, let alone fight again. But my father would have none of that. He informed my brother that the beating he would take at my father's hands would far outweigh anything that boy could dish out should my brother not go outside and whip that little white boys behind. My brother did what he was told.

In that instance, my father was undoubtedly attempting to teach my brother about respect. Demand respect. This man and his boy had come to our home and disrespected us, so they had to be dealt with. Thus, a little boy was made to fight another little boy for reasons that I'm quite sure neither of the boys could remember the next day. That little boy who came to the house with his father was probably forced to do so by his father. That father was surely trying to teach his son the same lesson. Respect. Who learned the lesson that day? This probably seems like a minor example, but a great many wars have been waged over respect. A man will use force to gain respect. What he actually gains is fear. This is a lesson I learned from working with juvenile delinquents. One can use force to get compliance, but the compliance is not out of respect. It is born from fear. Remove the physical threat and the compliance usually goes too. True respect, however, is gained through consistent and upright behavior. A man will fear a threat, because of the possibility of realizing the threat. A man will respect what he trusts to be true. Respect is far more valuable than fear because it requires very little energy to gain. With fear, one must constantly remind others of the threat. It loses its value over time. Real respect gains value.

Lesson #5

There is no lesson #5. Like so many men raised without a male role model, there are a great many lessons that I was never taught. Some of them are obvious. How to shave. How to hit a curveball. How to fish. My father wasn't around to teach me these things, and so I figured them out the best way I could. I learned to fish from my friend's father. I learned to shave through a rather painful trial and error process. I never did learn to hit a curve ball.

I can remember being a young boy playing baseball. I had raw talent. I was fast. I had good instincts. But, at some point, those things aren't enough anymore. Around the age of eleven or twelve, the better athletes start to separate from the pack. That's about the time those boys' fathers start to push them to go from good to great. My friends would be out on Saturday afternoons practicing with their fathers. Their dads were coaches. Their dads volunteered to help out. Their dads gave them extra instruction. Then there was me.

There were other things I never learned. How to approach a girl. How to treat her once you've approached her. The ins and outs of sex. A young boy doesn't realize that he doesn't know these things. It's difficult, at that young age, to have the insight to know what you don't know. It's only through the awkward process of life that a boy figures out that his previously infinite wisdom is often insufficient.

To this day, my ideas about women are confusing even to me. When I talk to women about the ideas that I have come to accept as reality about gender roles and relationships, most women are either amused or offended. I have often wondered where these ideas came from. As close as I can figure, I molded the memories and images of my parents' relationship into an idealized and unrealistic idea of what a relationship is supposed to look like. Because I was never told otherwise, I never had a reason to question my own thoughts. Until, that is, I had a relationship of my own to compare it to. When that happened, I slowly came to the realization that the relationship ideas that I had in my head only made sense in my head. Yet again, my lack of knowledge led directly to my inability to do the things that I so desperately wanted to do.

The Teacher

As I went about examining the lessons my father and society had taught me about manhood, I began to realize that there was another set of lessons that I lived by. I had never thought of them as manhood lessons but rather as life lessons. In fact, they can all be boiled down to one lesson. *Respect yourself.* Self-respect can mean a great many things. I had been taught this lesson in so many forms and in so many different situations that it had become the foundation and fabric of my existence. But I had never before thought of it as a "man" thing. Perhaps that's because a man didn't give it to me. This basic life lesson was given to me by my mother.

The funny thing is that I don't know that she ever actually spoke those words to me. Maybe she did, at one point or another. But what I do know is that she communicated that lesson to me over and over again in everything she taught me. That was my mother. Less talk, more walk. I suppose that's the way it has to be when you're a single mother of three young children. There's not a lot of time to sit and explain life when you're busy trying to live it. Many of the lessons I credit my mother with teaching me are lessons that she probably never consciously "taught."

I can remember going shopping at JcPenneys. We probably went shopping at other places, too. I think I only remember going to JcPenneys because the doors were heavy. It was my job to open those doors for my mother and for any other lady that was coming or going at the time I happened to be near the doors. As you might imagine, there are plenty of old ladies coming and going at a JcPenneys on a Saturday afternoon. But I opened those doors. If I didn't, my mother was there to remind me, sometimes nicely and sometimes not, that it was my job. If I remember correctly, I asked why once. The answer had something to do with me being young and strong and that a lady shouldn't have to open those doors when I was around. It didn't make much sense to me. Those doors were heavy for my eight-year-old arms. But questioning my mother's wisdom posed far more of a threat to me than the heavy doors, so I learned to open them. Similar logic was used when she taught me to walk on the outside of the sidewalk while in the company of a lady. She explained that, on occasion, a car would swerve onto the sidewalk. In the unfortunate event of such an accident, it was my job to take the hit, rather than allow the lady to be injured. I particularly remember thinking it was somehow strange that my mother would volunteer me to be struck by an oncoming car rather than some lady that I might be walking with. But I got the message. Treat a lady with respect.

The messages weren't always so simple. There were times when the lesson was harder to swallow. Being a young black boy where I grew up provided many opportunities to forget that I was a young *black* boy. Everyone grew up together. Not much distinction between black and white. Everyone went to school together. Everyone played together. So when we all became teenagers and started to date, it seemed reasonable that, as in everything else we'd ever done, there would be no distinction. Life quickly taught me otherwise.

There were a number of times when I would get the not-so-subtle message from a girl or her parents that I was less than welcome as a potential romantic interest in certain homes. I say romantic interest almost jokingly. After all, we're talking twelve-year-olds here. A romance between twelve-year-olds scarcely gets past holding hands and kissing occasionally. Still, it was often made clear to me that my hands and lips were outside of the acceptable limits of teenage romance. This fact, to me, was a minor consequence for being a part of the popular crowd. It never much fazed me. I always thought my mother to be above those parents who discriminated in this way. I never imagined that she'd bother to make such distinctions. That is, until I asked.

There was a particular girl, on one particular day, who wanted to come to my house for a visit. She and I thought this plan to be perfect. Her parents had said I was forbidden from her house, but they had, as yet, made no mention of restrictions upon *my* house. Thinking that my mother would understand this plan to be reasonable and fair, I asked my mother if I could have my friend over. Her response has stuck with me for the duration of my life. She asked, "Are you allowed to go to her house?" My answer was, of course, "No." "Then she isn't allowed at your house." A teenager at the time and far more brave than I was years earlier, I questioned her logic. Her explanation was simple: You should respect yourself enough not to invite someone into your home who would not invite you into theirs.

Then, there was the time that a group of my friends and I were at the local mall. Being a handful of young black boys proved to be problematic on more than one occasion. On this particular evening, a security guard took it upon himself to decide that although there was an ocean of teenagers flooding the mall at that moment, my group of friends needed special attention. We responded as you might imagine teenage boys would when they feel picked on.   Words were exchanged. We were expelled from the mall henceforth and forever. There were a handful of us that got kicked out of that mall, and we all went home and told our parents.   I don't remember the reaction that the others got, but I remember what I got. My mother first questioned my behavior. I assured her that, at first, we had done nothing wrong. Being black on a Friday night was still a misdemeanor in those days.   I admitted, though, that once we were kicked out of the mall, we expressed our displeasure at our unfair treatment using language that was unlikely to meet her approval. When I made that confession, I fully expected to be punished harshly. After all, my mother had raised me to respect elders just as I had been taught to respect women. I had also been forbidden to use any foul language whatsoever. But my mother's response in that moment was not anger. She didn't yell. She didn't spank me. She said, "We'll go see them in the morning. Tell your friends, if they want to come, they can." In my initial shock, I was sure that I had heard wrong. I just admitted to cussing, yelling, and disrespecting an adult authority figure in public. I somehow lived to tell the tale. Needing clarification, I asked if I was in trouble. She explained that if we had done nothing to be kicked out of the mall, we did not deserve the treatment we received. She was disappointed in my language, but she made this point clear: Never show respect to anyone who doesn't show respect to you.

The next morning came and, true to her word, my mother rounded up my friends and I. We went to that mall I had been expelled from the night before. For the first time, I witnessed what it truly meant to demand respect. My mother had the mall office gather the security staff. With my help, they identified the guard who had dealt with my friends and I the night before. In front of his colleagues, that guard got a tongue lashing the likes of which I'm quite sure he'd never taken from a stranger. No swearing. No threats of violence. Just a lady calmly letting them know which little boy they'd never be disrespecting again. The guard and his supervisor apologized, and we went on our way. For years after that day, I would see that guard at that mall and I would just smile. I never said a word. I didn't have to.

I could go on. Those lessons were just examples. This was the way it was with my mother. While my father had taught me to demand respect with my hands, my mother had taught me to demand respect with my mind. She would often say that I should never do anything that would embarrass her. I used to think this was a selfish request. I have come to realize that this was the greatest gift she ever gave me. At every turn, I had to decide whether or not my mother would approve. If I thought not, it was likely that the thing I was contemplating was a bad idea. I used to say that I was behaving well out of respect for my mother. I now realize that she had taught me to respect myself. My father would say never let anyone disrespect you or your family. My mother would say never disrespect yourself. It's a subtle distinction, but it makes all the difference in the world.

Applying the Lessons

As a young adult, I have often found myself in situations where I had to ask myself what my father would do. I used to use that as my barometer for manly behavior. But, as I said, somewhere along the way, I began to suspect that my father's wisdom was not perfect. One instance in particular sticks out. A man that I would have called a friend came to my house to have words with me. He had heard that I'd said things about his wife that he didn't think were kind. Unfortunately, he was right—I did. Our wives were friends. Angry with my wife one evening, I told her that she and her friend were both stupid. He heard about the remark and felt a need to defend her honor. He came to my house, presumably looking for a fight.

It's a funny thing, the laws of man. As was taught to me by my father, this guy was correct to defend his family. Still, when applying the laws of man, men often forget that the same laws bind both men. By my father's reasoning, a man had just come to my home with ill will in his heart and mind. There is only one solution to this problem. So, by the laws of man, you have two men who feel totally justified in beating each other silly. The question becomes who is more correct. And does it matter? Let's say he succeeds in provoking me to a fight and wins the fight. I was taught to fight to the death if need be. No doubt this guy was taught along the same lines. So, when the fight is over, who has won? One man is dead. The other goes to jail. Two wives widowed. Two sets of children left to learn these lessons alone.

The only logical answer came from my mother. If I respect myself, I won't stoop to the level of the fight. My family is more important to me than this argument. My need to be present for my family must come before my need to physically impose my will upon another man. When I calmly asked him to leave and told him I'd allow this incident to pass, his face showed his shock. He knew the rules. He may have expected a fight. He may have expected me to run in fear. He clearly didn't expect me to calmly demand respect just as my mother had that day at the mall.

I remember another instance when my father's ways didn't work for me. I was shopping with my daughter, something that we did often. At that time, I was working several extra shifts at work in order to make sure I had the money to fund those special shopping trips. My daughter turned to me that day and asked, "Dad, do you like work more than you like us?" It was as if she'd hit me with a ton of bricks. In my mind I was doing my job; I was providing. I was working 60 and 70 hours every week in order to give my family the things I thought they deserved. It's what my father had done. I never thought of it any other way. But all at once I saw that my daughter had no choice but to wonder where my priorities were. My actions were sending a message. As any child would, she would rather have spent time with her father than simply spend her father's money. My father had passed long before I could ask him why he was always at work, but my daughter was old enough to ask. Her question spoke volumes to me. That was not the first or the last lesson my daughter would teach me.

A Child is Born

They say that having a kid makes you grow up more quickly. I am here to tell you that this statement is not entirely true. When I was 17, I was a boy. That year, a child was born. The child's birth didn't magically change me into an adult. What did change me, though, was having a little girl watching me live my life. Maybe because of the way I was taught to see women, it felt like a special responsibility having a little girl. But, as I've said, I was still a boy when she was born, and much of what I now know about being a man, I hadn't learned yet.

I remember driving her around one day. She was about three or four years old. Just old enough to form sentences. Someone cut me off in traffic, and I reacted the way I normally would, "What the f #@k are you doing?" Then a little voice whispered from the back seat, "Why did you say that bad word?" It suddenly hit me: Someone was listening.

I remember having an argument with my wife one day. This was not odd. Before she was my wife, we argued. When she was my wife, we argued. Now that she's no longer my wife, we still argue. But the arguments changed at some point. See, before my baby girl was old enough to pay attention, I wasn't necessarily the nicest guy. But I remember arguing with her mother one day and thinking to myself that I had to at least be relatively nice. After all, my baby girl was listening. That's when life changed. That's when I realized that my job as her dad was to teach her what men look like, sound like, and act like. So, in order to do it right, I'd have to act like a man instead of a boy. Actions speak louder than words, right?

Over the years I have gotten better at it. And she has been there to point me in the right direction every step of the way. Not by saying so. She's still a kid. She doesn't even know she's directing my steps. But that little voice that I heard in the back seat of the car that day still rings in my head. Before I do any dumb boy thing that I might wish I could do, I always hear that voice saying, "Daddy why did you . . ." It's usually enough to talk me out of it.

Sonny Boy

As I said, I never understood the impact of a father until I had a son. My relationship with my daughter is one that is more reciprocal. I learn as much from being around her as she learns from being around me. There are only 17 years between us. I became a man in front of her eyes. In some ways, that's not ideal, but in some ways, it makes for a very special relationship. It's different with my son. He's young. He needs me in a different way. It's a kind of need that, until he was born, I didn't understand. He looks to me for all things male. I am his source for these things. Those lessons that I had to piece together in my father's absence are lessons that he fully expects to learn from me.

He doesn't always like the lessons I teach. In fact, one in particular is downright frustrating to him.

I often say to him, after he burps, or as he approaches those heavy doors without even attempting to hold them for his big sister, "Sonny boy, that's not the way a gentleman acts." He said to me once, "Dad, being a gentleman is hard work." He's right. It is hard work. It's even harder because his friends aren't raised that way. He goes to school and sees what his buddies are allowed to do, and then he comes home where he is held to a different standard. He doesn't understand why. It's possible that those are my father's expectations coming through, and that pressure for perfection is rearing its ugly head again. But there's also a basic truth in there. Respect yourself. Everything else will fall into place.

Because of the suddenness of my father's death, I often wonder what my son's life would be like if I were suddenly gone. What would he know? What questions would he have? What would I tell him if I were able to answer them? My father didn't leave me a manual. I wish he had. But if I had to write a manual for my son, what would it say? I fully intend to live long enough to teach him these lessons in person. Still, fear of repeating the past has compelled me to write my manual while I'm able. Maybe it's for him. Maybe it's for me. At any rate, here it is.

Part Three

Manhood: A Manual

First things first. Forget about the Laws of Man. They are a trick. Men will attempt to tell you what matters, but they will be wrong. They will say that men fight for principle. The truth is, men usually fight for pride. If you ever find yourself in a situation where you are considering fighting, emotionally or physically, for pride's sake, walk away. Whatever it is that is the root of the confrontation is likely to be something you will forget as time passes. Anything that can be forgotten is not worth fighting for.

Are there good reasons to fight? Sure. But those reasons will become obvious when they present themselves. When all other options have been exhausted, a man will defend himself and his family. The trick is knowing when all of the other options have been exhausted. If the consequence of a fight is worse than whatever it is that you are fighting for, that is a sure sign that you have not exhausted the options.

Rule #1: Respect Yourself

It seems like a simple thing. Respect yourself above all else. But in practice, it's not easy. When it feels as though others are disrespecting you, it is best to remember that it is impossible for anyone's behavior to affect you unless you allow it to. You can only control yourself. So, in any and every situation, you must remain in control of yourself. By doing so, you will avoid behavior that brings you any shame or dishonor. Men who fight and scream and behave badly in an attempt to demand respect often forget that doing so negates the intention of the act.

But self-respect goes far beyond avoiding a fight. It's in everything you do. It's in the way you treat a lady. It's in the way you speak to elders. It's in the way you do your work. If you hold yourself in the highest esteem, you will never forget to act in a way that will send that message to others. A self-respecting man could never be called lazy or rude. Why? He would never act in a way that would allow others to think that about him. Self-respect will not allow a man to be beneath anyone. A man stands upright in all his dealings. His walk commands respect from others. It's in his handshake. It's in the way he looks others in the eyes. It's in the way he holds his head up. Self-respect comes from the knowledge of one's worth. That's the key. When you accept that all men have infinite potential, there is a strength that comes from the respect for that potential. Greatness is your destiny. Act like it.

Rule #2: Remember Who You Are

Too often men are defined by what they do. A plumber gets a certain pride from fixing someone's pipes. When he does his job well, he feels good. But when he has a bad day, his worth is somehow in question because his identity is tied to his work. What happens when there are no drains to unclog? What happens when he doesn't get any work for weeks or months? He no longer has an identity that is relevant. But a man is not his work. I have met too many men who are fathers, sons, brothers, friends, and husbands. Men who love music and art. Men who have vast knowledge of a great many things. Somehow, though, because they have lost some job or because they don't do work that others find meaningful, they don't know who they are. It's as if their job is their only identifying feature, and when it's taken away, their manhood goes with it. But a man is not his job. A man is made up of his values, his interests, his knowledge, and his beliefs. His job is simply what he does. Never forget who you are. What you do should be a reflection of who you are, not vice versa.

Rule #3: Choose To Be Happy

Many people don't realize this, but happiness is a choice. Great men throughout history have said it. Glasser. Frankl. There are others. It's not a secret. Somehow, though, most people seem to ignore this basic truth. You will be as happy as you choose to be. The question is how do you do that? It's pretty simple: Only focus on the things that matter. Nothing that you can buy, sell, own, trade, or use really falls into this category. That's just stuff. Money is stuff. Houses and cars are stuff. Stuff comes and goes. Loved ones matter. Purpose matters. Beliefs matter. If you focus on the things that matter, you'll always have enough stuff. More accurately, you'll realize that there is no such thing as "enough" stuff, so there's really no point in calculating or measuring it.

People are often unhappy because they are focused on the *stuff* they don't have. I can speak from experience in saying that being broke is no fun. But an abundance of stuff won't cause happiness. Happiness comes from fulfillment. To be fulfilled in life, one must know what's important to him and do it. Whatever *it* is, do it. That's what purpose is. Purpose is that thing that makes you different than the guy standing next to you. My purpose is my children. They drive me. More broadly speaking, my purpose is all children. I focus on helping young people navigate the troubles that I've already seen, and it makes me feel happy.

If you can figure out why you are here, you'll know exactly what you need to do when you wake up everyday. That will make you happy.

Rule #4: Cry

Whoever said that a man isn't supposed to cry was wrong. That idiot messed it up for a great many men for years to come. We are told that real men don't cry. The real message is that men don't have emotions, and that emotions equal weakness. The opposite is true. Depth of emotion is a strength that men rob themselves of in an attempt to live up to some imaginary standard. It only hurts us. The ability to feel and express emotion gives us the ability to learn life's lessons. So cry when you need to. Laugh when you want to. Remember that anyone who tells you otherwise is just jealous of your freedom to feel these things. When you become numb to life, you cease to live.

Rule #5: Dream Big

There is a line in a song that says, "You gotta have a dream. If you don't have a dream, how you gonna have a dream come true?" This statement should be plastered on billboards the world over. This world is filled with little boys in little towns. They look out at the world and all its wonders and think, "That's not my life. That can't be me." But why not? Michael Jordan wasn't born "Michael Jordan." He was just a scrawny kid named Mike that wanted to play some ball. The only difference between him and all the other little boys is that he had that dream and a willingness to work tirelessly toward it. That's all it takes. Nothing more and nothing less.

Look at any great man. Deep inside every one of them is a little kid with a dream. You might see the finished product, but trust me; at the beginning of that journey was a kid just like you. Greatness is never an accident. It is not a birthright. It is never happenstance. Greatness, like happiness, is a choice. So dream big. Anything less is just a waste of time.

Ready, Go!

By conventional reasoning, I shouldn't be where I am. With all that I've been through, most people would not have expected me to end up where I have. I tell you this only to suggest that a happy, healthy life has nothing to do with your circumstances or surroundings. The stuff that happens to you is just stuff that happens to you. You are whatever you make of that stuff. Life will break you if you let it. Don't let it.

That's it.   That's all I've got.   In my
short life, these are the lessons I've learned.
I learned them from life.   I learned them
from my mother.   I learned them from
Victor Frankl and Ralph Emerson. I learned
them by making mistakes.   It's not
everything, I'm sure. If life has taught me
anything, it's that I don't know much.   So
pay attention and keep learning, because
knowledge really is power.   Perhaps when
I'm 80 years old, I'll know more.   Maybe
I'll disagree with some of what I've said
here.   Don't take my word for it.   Go live.
Let me know how it goes.

Peace and Love,
Dad